Two thousand copies
of this book
have been printed
and bound.

———————————————————

This is copy number *1470*

Gray's Journal

The Second Collection
by Ed Gray

Illustrations by Russell Buzzell

1984
Gray's Sporting Journal
South Hamilton, Massachusetts

This book is dedicated to
the Subscribers to
Gray's Sporting Journal

International Standard Book Number 0-9609842-2-4
Library of Congress Catalog Card Number 84-082448
Printed in The United States of America
Published by Gray's Sporting Journal Incorporated
205 Willow Street
South Hamilton, Massachusetts 01982

Contents

Imprint

I first saw the tracks ten years ago, mixed tracks in the sand where Bog Brook sweeps around the alder thicket before sluicing into Indian Stream. Letting the little Squirrel Tail ride in the current, I followed a set of the wider prints with my eyes as they left the river to vanish into the thick grasses on the other side. The flood plain isn't wide there and the ground turns quickly upward through balsams to a steep slope of hardwoods ending in the ridge, the rich line of spruce drawing an evening horizon, cold, untouched and whisper-quiet in the soft breath of a June north wind.

That's where they are, I said.

I'll come back, I said. In the fall, with Jeffrey and Mac. That's it.

It seemed so easy, so definite there with my feet firmly set in the rush of Bog Brook, my eyes drawn by the spruce ridge, and the only thing calling me away the insistent tug of a downstream Squirrel Tail. So easy that at first I didn't notice that the years were slipping by and we hadn't gone back.

Oh, no, not this year, Mac would say. There's this lady in Vermont, and you ought to see the grouse cover out behind her house . . .

Oh, no, not this year, Jeffrey would say. Why should I drive all the way up there when I've got all the deer I want right here near home . . .

And pretty soon I stopped asking. Stopped asking, but didn't stop dreaming. Didn't stop planning. And not once in the eight years that went by did I lose the vision of the ridgetop, the ragged dark edge of it pulling just up and over into the long country of the north, far expanse of unbroken treetops, a distant high bog, and not a single road for as far as you could see. I knew it would be that way.

8

It was that way, two years ago, when I asked Larry if he wanted to go. Sure, he said. Just like that. And on a very dark dawn in the third week in November we stepped off the woods road and into the balsams sloping up to the high ridge.

Three days later we left, and we had no deer. But we had had three days on the mountain, days of the deep woods with no other hunters, days of wide-splayed buck tracks in new snow, white flags bounding away through dense blowdowns, a hasty, missed shot apiece, and quiet hours up near the ridge that tailed away into the long country of the north. And when we came away, we came with a knowledge of the mountain that you could put in the bank. Next year . . .

Next year, last year, was the year.

On the first morning out, an hour after light in the deep grey of November after an all-night dusting of wet snow, nine and a half years after I first saw them, and spread wide and deep across the peak of the ridge itself, I saw the tracks again.

Not, of course, the same tracks, you say.

You say.

I say that I never left them. That from the time I first saw them stepping lightly away from Bog Brook those tracks were only accidentally out of my range of vision. That every time I sneaked into the crowded deer woods in the southern part of the state, every time I saw the hurried prints of a driven deer, I knew, knew it just had to be, that those prints would slow on the other side of the hill. Would slow, and gain poise and power as they turned north. Would widen, and gain depth in the unhurried stride of the north woods buck. Would slow, and be drawn, just as I was, to the ridge, dark-spruce chimera only next year away. For nine years, only next year away.

So when I saw the prints, sharp-edged in three inches of new snow, wide-set with drag marks toeing in, I knew them. And when I knelt to feel the compressed snow in one of them, all of those times past, dreams and plans come and gone, quietly went away, rushed all together down the hill to wait in silence in the cabin below.

Without any of them, alone on the mountain and without fantasy for the first time in nine years, I stood up to follow

9

the tracks. Focussed and becoming clear, I moved with them.

The tracks led across the last of the white oak tablings, straight and with purpose. I had learned the year before not to look for rubs or scrapes in the hardwoods. Not on this ridge, where all the rut-stands get marked in spruce edges. I cut across the flat part, and climbed the little granite face on the other side, sure that the tracks would appear again on the higher part.

For me, this is the best part of deer hunting—a considered risk, leaving the fresh track, guessing where it should go, shortening the distance to the deer. He's probably just up there, you tell yourself, just over the lip and moving away. Be careful now.

Be careful now in the downed spruces along the top. Take quiet care sliding over the big ones, slip gently around the snow-thickened balsams. The track is there, you know it.

There it is, just ahead and moving right. Follow it now as it crosses the ridge and heads down. Very, very slowly now; don't look any more at the track, look up now ahead to where the trees aren't trunks, to where the forest fades and blends dark at the far range of your woods vision.

Stop now. There is no noise. Something.

Something moving. Dark grey shape gliding down there, a hundred yards. There, now behind the trees. There is no noise.

Nothing to see now. Just feel it, feel it coming. Rifle slowly, slowly up.

The shape again, between the dark trunks, gone again. Closer, and now you see it will be fifty yards when you see it again. There is no noise.

A breath now, it's here, right here. The world is a cone, forty yards, right behind those trees. A motion. Twig snap.

Antlers.

It was, for me, as long as tracks get, and I doubt that I'll find as completely rounded a finish on another. But every year they get wider, these prints that start on the ground, wander into my spirit and lead me through time. There's never an end to them, not even to the buck track above Bog Brook.

Because, you see, when I was up there, quietly trailing the buck across the high ridge, I stood and looked out across the long country. And away to the north, glistening bright in the late morning sun, was the gentle curve of a beaver-dammed brook whose name I didn't know. Lying hidden in the far sweep of a roadless valley, even in November it seemed the perfect place for a June Squirrel Tail.

That's where they are, I said.

September, 1978

Thank You, New Hampshire

I'm an out-of-state hunter. Not that there isn't good hunting right here at home, there is. It's just that I like to go where the birds are in the right place, and for me ruffed grouse are in the right place when they're in New Hampshire.

You see, the first grouse I ever saw was in New Hampshire; the first several that I missed with my then unfamiliar 16-gauge were in New Hampshire, and when I finally shot one, the bird fell in an old orchard in the Granite State.

Now I know that Minnesota has more grouse, and that good coverts are more predictable in Ohio. It doesn't matter. For me, for grouse hunting, New Hampshire is home.

It was there, while I was in graduate school at Dartmouth, that my friend Mac started me hunting. Mac, who had been raised to rod and gun, knew just how to hook me, and he did it two ways. First, he loaned me a shotgun and took me to the hills near Hanover, and then he gave me his copy of *The Old Man and the Boy.*

I haven't been the same since.

Those days afield, in October, in New Hampshire, and the evenings adrift with Ruark, in boyhood—can you imagine the effect it had on me? It was pure magic.

And much of that magic was the grouse. For I didn't find very many that first year, and I didn't shoot a single one; it seemed that I was just getting the hang of it when the season closed and the woods were full of deer hunters. (But I had learned the lay of the land that first partridge season, so that when Mac loaned me his 30-30, I got my deer on the back side of one of our grouse coverts.)

Before I could get back to those grouse coverts, I had to make my peace with Uncle Sam, and he said that a couple of years in uniform in Virginia would do the trick. I agreed, made the best of it, and when I came back to New Hampshire, I brought my friend, Whit, a yearling golden retriever who, until he got to New England, thought that game birds came only in coveys and spent their time at the edges of soybean fields.

That was the year that we both learned the difference, and that was the year that New Hampshire and grouse became forever inseparable in my view of things.

I'm sure that Whit and I spent more days afield that season than in any since, or at least it seems that way. At first we went out with Mac and with Jeffrey, my oldest friend and another of Mac's novitiates; often it was the four of us—Mac leading us to the covert, Jeffrey and I on the flanks, and Whit, nose to the ground and tail wildly rotating, pitching into the ground cover. It was quite a show, but we learned fast that this was not the way to hunt grouse—the few birds that held long enough to get up in gun range were met with a fusillade which transfixed the dog and always led to extended negotiations over who had actually hit the bird.

So Whit and I began more and more to go out alone. It was far better; we could go when we wanted and pick our own places, and we began to explore.

The first time we went out alone we discovered the old cemetery way up behind the Skiway, lost on a dead end and hidden from the road by dense junipers. Later we found the beaver flow with the black ducks in it. Together we followed the worn bear-run on the back of Moody Mountain, and we shared lunch by an ancient cellar-hole in a field overlooking Indian Pond. And every single time we found grouse. Literally every time. I didn't always hit them, but we never failed, on those times alone, to move at least one bird.

Of course it hasn't been that way since—just that one season in New Hampshire, when Whit and I learned to hunt alone.

It was a good season, but short, as New Hampshire seasons are. Near the end we put a cap on it with a day that will always stand alone.

It was the last day of our four-day trip to the College Grant near Errol. There, living in a cabin in Dartmouth's wilderness tract, thirteen miles back from the macadam, Jeffrey, Mac,

Whit and I hunted hard in coverts where the grouse are seldom disturbed. Three days later, after miles of alder runs, blueberry thickets, and birch-whip edges, we had moved only a few birds, and we hadn't killed one. The fourth day it rained.

It was one of those fine-misted, all day rains that are so common in that country, and it was cold. Jeffrey and Mac decided to stay in the cabin, keeping the fire going and enjoying the solitude of 40 square miles of wet woodland. Whit and I went grouse hunting.

I knew that we had to leave early the next day, that the season would shortly be over, and that we would be leaving New Hampshire in the spring—I wasn't going to give up. Whit knew none of these things, he just wanted to hunt, so we spent the whole day alone, in the woods.

I don't know how much ground we covered, or precisely where we went that day; Whit's nose led the way, and occasionally I steered us toward better-looking cover. In the late afternoon, birdless, we came back to the road three miles above the cabin. The fine mist was still coming down, and I had given up hope of moving anything. Whit was exhausted and stayed at a loose heel while we walked back toward Mac and Jeffrey and the fire.

About a mile from the cabin, at a corner where an old logging slash met the road, Whit stopped, looked toward the slash, twitched his nose, and dove into the cover. Five grouse got up.

I shot two of them. Whit picked them up one at a time, brought them to me, and, just like that, we had a memory.

Now, whenever I think of New Hampshire, I smell woodsmoke from an all day fire in a Franklin stove, there's a bourbon in my hand, a wet dog asleep on the floor, and two grouse are hanging on the porch of a cabin in the Dartmouth College Grant. The nearest road is thirteen miles away, and it's raining.

This year I'm going back, because I try to go back whenever I can, and because this year New Hampshire has given me a present. For the first time since I left New Hampshire, the state has issued a special non-resident bird hunting license.

I'm glad that the state has realized that some of us out-of staters don't hunt deer there, and I'm glad that they've made it easier for some of us to come home again.

You see, a non-resident isn't always a stranger.

October, 1975

Purpose

One tends to think of trout fishing as the gentlest of field sports, reserving the adjectives "thrilling" and "dangerous" for big game hunting and some types of offshore fishing. The trout fisherman, in the classic picture, usually releases the few fish he takes, and the trout, in their turn, provide the angler with pleasant companionship on quiet rivers far removed from the life-and-death struggles each has to face at other times and other places.

It's all very civilized, very refined and, for me, all wrong. Like so many human pursuits, this one tends too much toward the cerebral, with too many artificial rules, too many calculated restrictions, until in its "perfection" the game becomes too far removed from its original, and now obscure, intent.

I treat my trout fishing as I treat the other things that I do when I go out—always conscious of the difference between fishing and catching, I go to my trout waters without much forethought, expecting nothing in particular and everything in general. That way, the things that do happen are somehow more enjoyable, and more often it's in the little occurrences that I find clues to that long-lost intent.

Early in the season a few years back we camped for several days on a nice little river, and spent most of the time trying to keep small brookies off the sparse streamers we swung in front of their elders. On the final day I was down to my last Squirrel Tail, and it was the only fly that worked. There was a deep undercut run across the stream, and, keeping my backcast high, I neatly planted that precious lure high in the alders on the far side.

Now one of the reasons that I fish with fine tippets is that it makes it easier to yank the line out of trees, but this time

I couldn't afford to leave the fly on a branch. Edging cautiously toward the dropoff, I could just reach the fly with the tip of my rod; concentrating intently, I looped the tip-top over the hook and pulled sharply.

I suppose the Squirrel Tail is still in that tree—I don't really know, since the only thing that gave way on that sudden jerk was the gravel under my feet. Water poured in over my wadertops, and five knots of mountain freshet pulled me under.

As I went down, I lunged at the bank and grabbed an overhanging alder trunk and hung on. Oh, I know that Lee Wulff says that you can't drown in waders, that you should relax and ride down to shallow water—especially in small streams, but, as I understand it, he practiced in swimming pools. And besides, he wasn't down to his last Squirrel Tail.

Of course, I made it, and dragged myself up the bank, now on the wrong side of the river; but in the action I had broken my rod tip, lost my favorite hat, and my creel had opened and three trout had slipped forever downstream.

Another time, and this story's a little more sinister, Frank and I were casting into openings in the ice for early season landlocked salmon. The day was raw and windy, the season barely open, and we held out little hope of eliciting a strike. But it had been a long winter, and we wanted to do some casting.

We were trying to get our streamers out toward the ice's edge, and it was a pretty long cast. The wind was coming from our right and it puffed just as Frank grunted out his final backcast on a long double-haul; even in the wind you could hear the Thwack! as the fly hit him in the face.

When he turned around, the streamer was hanging from his eyelid, firmly embedded with the barb having gone all the way in and back out again. I gently clipped the leader and drove Frank to the hospital, where the doctor said that the eye had not been punctured—the fly had only gone into his eyelid. But the doctors were worried that further aggravation of the bruised eye would permanently cloud Frank's vision, so they put patches over both eyes and made him lie tranquilized in a hospital bed for a month.

Frank recovered all right, but because he was flat on his

back he wasn't along on what turned out to be my favorite trout fishing experience.

Jeffrey and I were fishing the Dead Diamond River, and on the third day of our stay we decided to hike upriver a few miles to the really untouched portion. It was a lovely June morning, the river susurrant through the pines, with occasional glimpses of Magalloway Mountain and the fire tower as we walked the tote road upstream.

The river was smaller up there, but it still had enough water to hold some good fish. Jeffrey and I fished several pools and most of the fast water, taking turns at the smaller runs and casting together where there was room. Toward midafternoon the weather turned hot and muggy; I was upstream and around a bend from Jeffrey.

It had been an idyllic afternoon, easy and slow-paced, and I was captivated in the quiet rhythm of cast-and-float, retrieve-and-cast . . .

Boom!

It was the loudest thunderclap I've heard yet—I looked up just as driven rain and rolling black clouds came roaring down the little valley. It was stupefying, the windnoise overpowering all else, and lightning began to strike on both sides of the river. Trees came crashing down in the adjacent woods, and I cringed against the bank, not daring to get out into the trees, frightened at the thought of standing in water in an electrical storm—there was nowhere to go, nothing to do.

And very quickly the storm passed. Shivering and wet, I made my way down to where Jeffrey had been; he, too, had stayed in the river, and when I found him he was wide-eyed, speechless, with a faint smile just starting as he saw me come downriver.

We didn't say anything on the way back to the cabin. There was no need to—the point had been clearly made. In a lifetime of surprises afield, this had been the biggest, the one that had most effectively squeezed us both into our obviously small niches in the grand scheme.

For me, this gets right to the point of it all. We're all seeking something when we get out there—one man may say he's seeking solitude, another will say that he wants to clear his head a bit, and you may just be looking for a brown trout.

Each of these stated goals is euphemistic, a metaphor for that which drives us all, and whose true name none of us knows.

Me, I keep looking for the clues. And it's in the unexpected that they always turn up.

March, 1976

Harmony

I prefer bass water to all else.

Give me 15 or 20 acres of quiet water, a canoe and a good selection of topwater lures, and I'll leave the rest of the world alone for a week. I'll poke along very slowly, looking in the waterweeds for duck nests and painted turtles, watching bluegills and redears dart away from the shadow of the gliding canoe, and listening to the stentorian bravado of the bullfrogs.

I won't even pick up a rod until a redwing blackbird, perched lightly on a cattail, draws me to the proper bushy point. Then I'll cast a small, yellow popping bug up underneath the bird, just to see what happens. Most likely the bug will rest there, motionless, until I give the line as delicate a twitch as I can—just enough to send a ripple radiating out from the little yellow lure and into the cattails.

If I haven't scared the redwing, he'll cock his head at the movement below, and hop to another reed while the popping bug stutters its way out toward the canoe. As long as the bird stays near, I'll keep casting near him, but if he flies away, I'll look for another spot. There's nothing scientific in this—I just like to do it that way.

And I'll take care to work each of the casts all the way back to the canoe, so a following bass will come close enough for me to see. The bass will stop a few feet away and we'll watch each other for a minute, then he'll swim away. I used to worry about the bass seeing me like that, thinking that the fish would be spooked and that I'd have to find another spot and another bass. Now I know better.

I know I began to get a sense of it late in May on Goose Pond, several years ago. I had paddled my canoe across to where the early season high water created an island out of what was, for the rest of the year, a small peninsula. I knew that large smallmouths and pickerel gathered in the shallows to prey upon the baitfish seeking cover in the grasses of the flooded causeway, and the year before I had taken a 25-inch pickerel there from two feet of water.

It was late in the afternoon, the fishing was slow, and I was idly watching my deer-hair mouse drift soggily past a deadfall. There was a loud crashing in the woods, the noise sounding like a series of trees falling, each one closer to the shore, fifty feet to my right. Then a panicked doe came bounding to the shoreline. The deer looked quickly over the water, her eyes pausing on me for the briefest of moments, and she swam out into the pond. When the shoreline, and her pursuer, were thirty feet behind, she turned and swam along the shore and kept swimming until she was out of sight, a quarter of a mile or so around a point of land.

I don't know whether or not I caught any fish that day, but I do remember the deer. For just that fractured second, I was in harmony, and the unknown in the woods was not. A simple, probably commonplace event—yet, for me, it was like the proverbial lightbulb flicking on.

After that it was easy. Maybe it had been there all along and I just hadn't noticed it, but there was no mistaking it now: The residents of a bass pond were never surprised at seeing me. While I fished, they'd go about the business of being a turtle or minnow, mallard or dragonfly, without any visible disruption of the communal ethos. The languid predation went on at all levels, and the gentle ripples from my bass bug were nothing more than another part of the random pattern that made up the whole.

I thought of the dread and artificial silence of the deer woods, of snapped twigs and the violent scolding of blue jays and red squirrels, where a windblown chance of a man-scent sends cautious animals scurrying over ridgetops. Or the painstaking care with which I had to approach a trout pool, where an errant shadow or a dropped flyline stills the water for half an hour. The frozen indecisiveness of a covey of quail in front of a man with a dog. A saltmarsh emptying of geese at the approach of a small boat. Everywhere had I known wild things viewing me with alarm, hiding, running or flying from me.

But not on the bass pond. Oh, I know that the blue heron

will ponderously squawk away, and the kingfisher will chatter and dip from tree to tree down the shore—but only if you get too close, and not at the distant sight of your boat. No, most of the time you'll fit right in without a break in the pattern. Don't ask me why this is so—it's just the way that it works on a bass pond.

Or on a bass lake. Last summer Becky and I spent a long weekend camped on the shore of my favorite smallmouth water; it's a long drive to where we put in the canoe, and by the time we had paddled to the campsite it was getting dark. We quickly pitched the tent, built a fire, and were just finishing a cup of coffee when we heard heavy footsteps behind the tent, in the gloom just outside the firelight.

"There's somebody out there," said Becky, but I knew better. I guess I just shed the city faster than she did—it had been a pretty abrupt change—and besides, I was on a bass lake. When we stood up, there was much rhythmic crashing through the alders, and the next morning the moose's tracks were bigger than Becky's hand.

Another herbivorous lightbulb, it was a perfect foretoken for the trip. For the next three days we enjoyed good weather, fast fishing, and the feral ambiance of a lake in Maine. We spent one morning with a nesting loon, first watching from a distance, then following her as she led us from the eggs with a water-flailing, broken wing act. We watched a bald eagle catch a thermal and rise out of sight, and we pitched small surface lures in among the dri-ki, where the wakes of foraging pickerel quietly rocked the rotted branches of dead spruce trees. The moose didn't come back, but he wasn't far away, probably just out of view and up the feeder stream a ways, at the marshy bend where the osprey builds his nest.

You see, we were on bass water, where, better than any other place I know, you'll find Thoreau's invisible companion.

May, 1976

Full Count

For me, the strike is the thing. I'll admit to some pretty comfortable feelings about actually putting a good one in the net, but I'll never get used to the Pop! of a fish hitting what I've put out there.

It's not just the unexpected nature of it, and it's not the gratification of outwitting him; to tell the truth of it, I rarely feel as if I've outwitted a fish, but rather that by continued casting I've increased the probability of that heart-flushing Pop! Now if by carefully placing a plug right against a dead-fall, or through proper mending of a flyline bowed by a fast center current, I can increase that probability, then that's fine. But the point is that when the fish does hit, the excitement is at the fish's end of the line, not mine.

It's all a matter of concentration. When you're really into it, all of your faculties are focused on the lure. If it's a surface plug or a dry fly, then you mostly watch, but if you've cast something that sinks, then you've got to imagine—and you've got to travel right down the line to where all that wobbly, quick predatory stuff is going on. It's almost asking too much of yourself; like keeping your eyes open in the shower scene in *Psycho*, or not gripping the safety bar on the steep part of a roller-coaster.

Maybe that's why I prefer to use surface lures, something that I've carried to an extreme in my inshore salt water fishing. The minute-to-minute tension is less, because you can see the lure, and when the fish does strike, the moment is far more intense. It's probably one of those personal oddities, but I know the precise second that I developed the preference:

It was in early October on the south shore of Cape Cod, during the tail-off of a three-day southwester. The wind was gusting at around 20 knots while bulky dark clouds scudded down the widening reach of Cotuit Bay, and cold rain was pelting down in sheets across the marsh just north of the nearly empty anchorage. In the summer this was an almost tritely picturesque holding spot for daysailers and yachts bobbing painted-fresh at moorings that had people's names on them; but after Columbus Day you could hitch an old Whaler to any of them and be alone for the rest of the day. Especially on a day like this.

Of course I like to spend some time near the fireplace and watch the weather go by, and this probably would have been a good day for it. But for two days I had been trying steadily to do something that I had never done. Catch a striped bass.

A modest goal, to be sure; one that most of the fishermen in that part of the world had accomplished very early on in their experience. Not me. I was beginning to feel about the bass the way that my pal Mac had come to view grouse—after a couple of very barren seasons, he started looking for a Grouse Tag on his hunting license and took to asking you if you had "gotten your grouse yet" as the season progressed.

Stripers are pretty easy to pick up if you troll the tidal rips offshore, and in the early and late seasons they are mixed in with the bluefish off Popponesset Beach. But I wanted to do it the right way, and for me the right way was to cast an Atom Popper from an open boat anchored in the shallower bay.

I didn't get around to giving it a serious effort until that October, and I probably shouldn't have been so certain that success would come on that particular weekend. But that's the best month, and even as strong as it was, a southwest wind was just right. And I like the rain.

Actually the rain didn't come until that third day. For the previous two I had contended only with the wind and my own frustration. Mostly I had fished alone in the bay, but the previous afternoon a man came by in an old Lyman lapstrake, and in one half-mile drift took two stripers with a fly rod. He hadn't said anything as I watched him take the two fish, and I maintained what I thought was a laconic, professional deference. When he left, he swung the old boat near and over the wind he confided, "Use a white one!"

White *what*? My Atom Popper weighed more than his fly

24

rod, and anyway, it was two-toned baby blue and white with metal flakes in it, the way you might paint the gas tank on a Norton Atlas. I did have some all-white lead-head jigs, and I messed around with them for a while, trying to imitate the action of a 2/0 streamer, but there was little hope there. I switched back to the plug and fruitlessly cast until dark.

On the third day I wondered at the timing of fish migrations and had visions of my bass now all gone from the Cape and making serious progress toward the wintering grounds off Oregon Inlet at Hatteras. But I calmed myself with the re-assurance that I was fishing as much for a method as I was for a fish, and that I could be a success without a bass. So I turned my back to the weather, and as the rain rattled off my slicker and ran down my legs and into my shoes, I made long downwind casts and syncopated, sputtering retrieves.

I didn't then know what a mantra was, and I'm not com-pletely clear on it now, but what I had working that day in Cotuit Bay was a lot like that. *Take* the lure, *take* the lure, *take* the lure . . . Steady, rhythmic, thought-banishing, your self confined and held by the imbuement of the weather, and your total concentration on the little blue-and-white flaky thing in the water; the act becoming dance, the dance be-coming self-sufficient . . .

Pop! Disjointingly sudden, splash against the wind, flash of arched silver . . . a bass! Gone under now, line singing off the reel, but beyond doubt a bass. I eased the drag and held the rod up, but my mind was held, back there at the strike. The fish tugged and surged and all I could see was the strike. The flash, the sudden moment of it.

Eventually the fish tired and I picked him up with the long-handled net and put him in the boat. For a long time I stared at the thing there; green along the back, silver on the sides, two spiny dorsal fins, eight black stripes, a gold eye. Twenty inches long and about five pounds. It was beautiful, and as if to make it more so, I said so out loud. I said it again, and it didn't work. I just could not move the prize ahead of the challenge, the catch ahead of the strike.

It's years later and I've caught lots of bass. I moved to lighter and lighter tackle, then to the fly rod, and when Jeffrey was tying salt water streamers one winter he tied me a "white one" and it works. In fact, it works better than the poppers that I use, but it's not very often out of the wallet—I just can't get away from using topwater lures. I just don't ever want to miss seeing the strike.

Nor do I want to miss seeing the quail flush, the teal set his wings, or the marlin slap the teaser. It's all the same thing.

It's the unifying event when, from out of the weather and the ocean, from out of the forest and field, and from the very passage of time itself, something out there *strikes*.

And you caused it.

July, 1976

Appearances

For most of us, weather is important to our hunting. For me, it's critical.

Weather. It really is the whole thing. Weather is what causes the birds to be where they are at the moment, and for some years now it has been the windowgazing insistence that orders the events of my Fall.

It's all a matter of matching the bird to the place—and the place isn't the same from month to month. An old apple tree sunning itself in an overgrown raspberry thicket with butter-flies flitting up into the blue warmth of August is not a grouse covert. Blow the leaves away, knock down the fruit so that it can ferment and rot a bit on the ground, brown-freeze the low grasses and cover the whole business with the brooding grey of coming snow—*then* you'll find birds in there, you can count on it.

This view of birds, places, and the proper time to hunt them goes a lot deeper than just fond memories of seasons past; it's a considered outlook that sits at the very core of my being out there in the first place.

I think that I began to move so closely with the weather when I began to hunt woodcock.

For my first few seasons among them, woodcock were the odd whistling frustrations that came up from what was sup-posed to be a grouse run. I didn't intentionally seek woodcock coverts, and only found the birds when a cold wind drove them into the places where Whit and I sought other birds. The dog would get very birdy in a good covert, and right at the tremulant height of it this airy, flapping feather with a long nose would daintily aviate into the puckerbrush.

Of course, I never hit them. Only rarely did I shoot at them—it was just too confusing, too unexpected for grouse-ready synapses to handle. It took an odd turn of the weather, and Whit's best-ever dog work, to re-order my priorities forever.

For over a week it had rained steadily, and on the first passable day Whit and I went hunting. When we got to the covert only the higher spots were without standing water. Most of the adjoining alder runs were too wet to work through, and pretty quickly Whit and I got to the edge of what seemed to be the good part. Not a bird.

Whit gets anxious in scenes like this, and while I was surveying the swale and debating the possibility of decoying a wood duck or two, he lurked off into the drowned alders. As soon as I realized that the dog had vanished I went into my voice-hoarsening act, and after ten minutes or so out he came. Slowly, truly hang-dog, and there was something in his mouth that he would not drop.

Whit had had an absurd dance with a porcupine the year before, and I thought that he might have resumed the step, but as he got closer it became clear that there were no quills in his mouth.

There was a woodcock in his mouth. I didn't know that woodcock could drown, and while I was puzzling this out I called 'fetch' to the dog. Sheepishly he came and put the bird at my feet. It flew away. Sort of.

Jerkily and fluttering it went out over the open grass, and when it got 25 yards or so out there I shot it. Whit splashed over the the spot, picked up the woodcock, and sat down. I called 'fetch' and he sat there. *No way, boss—come and get it this time.*

Even though it was my first woodcock and was, therefore, the beginning of a more rational relationship between us, I'm sorry that I shot that bird because it was the only chance I expect in which I'll have the opportunity to throw one back. Not really, but as close as you can come outside of fishing or live-trapping, and I think that I would have liked to see if there might be anything to it.

Whatever the latent effect of this illaudable event, I do know that I then began seriously to hunt woodcock, and as I learned the habits of the bird I became slowly aware of his most appealing characteristic: He doesn't arrive in the uplands until I do.

Grouse, pheasant and quail are there all year, and the dove cruises through in the heat of the late summer. None of these birds shares my addiction to the somber grey of a late-October afternoon when the wind carries some North in it, and long-dead leaves pile against the stone fences of a high pasture in New England.

But the woodcock does. That's the day that will find him moving into the alders, or into the light hardwoods above the streambed. The grouse will be unhappily roosted in the high spruce and the holdover pheasant will have gone deep into the old beaver bog, hunching testily under the bull-briars, immovable.

It will be three in the afternoon on a day when shooting light will fail by four. Snow will probably come that night, and already the dank cold of it seeps past the rubber and wool to my toes. Whit is tired and mud-darkened from the lower coverts of hours ago, and I find myself carrying the twenty gauge over my shoulder in places where I should be more alert. There might be a bird in the game pocket; might not. We're pretty far from the car, and woodsmoke is coming from the farmhouse down in the hollow. The dog is slow now, only tentatively casting to either side as we come to the heavier growth at the far end of the field.

And then Whit comes to life. His nose jerks him forward, tail high and into the cover. Just as I get the gun off my shoulder there's a whistling flurry back in there where I can't see. Gun up, foot forward, looking, looking . . .

The pattern is always right with the woodcock, and with the weather. I don't know who the weaver is, but I do know that he keeps putting me in there with them both.

September, 1976

Sieve

Most of us are less than two hours away from some kind of deer cover. Finding a red hat and some .30-30 rounds isn't much of a chore, and after that the only obstacle is your circadian resistance to a four a.m. alarm.

With other forms of big-game hunting it's a different story. Only the lucky ones can knock off a half-day's work and go elk hunting; the usual first step in setting up for stone sheep or caribou is the purchase of airline tickets or drawing lots for the dog-watch shift on a three-day enduro in Fred's car. Add in the guides, lotteries, heavy provisioning and unfamiliar hunting territory and the nature of the hunt gets pretty far removed from the bare-bones simplicity of the deer woods.

This comparison is not new, and a lot of conclusions have been drawn from it, but for me the essential point is familiarity. If I travel to the Coquihalla Mountains and am lucky enough to pluck a mountain goat from the local herd, I'll remember that hunt in detail for a good long time, but I suspect that the experience will rate closer to high entertainment than it will to a chapter heading in my book of days.

But if, in the early morning of a hard-frost November day this fall, I draw a slow bead on the buck I know on the back side of Whitcomb Mountain, it's going to be the accumulation of years of decisions that will urge me to pull the trigger. In fact, it will have been a fair number of yellow-dappled forks that get me to Whitcomb Mountain in the first place.

I'll be hunting there because it's pretty far back off the road and I'm sure no one else will be on the hill with me unless I've invited him along for the hunt. It's important that I be alone—alone and careful, quiet in the woods—because of a deal I made with myself ten years ago.

Ten years ago Mac lent me his rifle and I went deer hunting

for the first time. At odd times during the three-week season I would get out into the woods around Hanover, and with two days left in the season I shot my deer. On the back side of the Skiway, at three in the afternoon, and it took me five shots to do it.

I had found the jeep trail early in the grouse season; there hadn't been many birds there and it didn't occur to me until that late day that deer might be there. It had snowed earlier in the week and the trail was a crusted three inches; I was making so much crunching noise walking up that at first I didn't believe it when I saw the deer standing in the trail 75 yards in front of me. His, or her, head was out of sight in the bush to the left, but the whole body was clear and broadside; it's either sex in New Hampshire, so I lined up and fired— offhand, sling tight, exhale and squeeze. The deer bolted into the cover.

I bolted into the cover. The deer was bounding down a small ravine; I tried to lead it and fired again, missed again, and the deer went out of sight over the lip of the other side.

The shot noise still echoed in the hardwoods when the second deer appeared, following the first one and moving fast. Again I tried to track and fire, and again I missed. Twice. And as soon as this deer went over the lip, the third one appeared, in the track and following. I just watched it go.

And then the fourth deer came, stepping quietly in the track while I watched. Halfway down the little draw, the deer stopped. It was 50 yards away; I held the rifle stock against a tree and shot it.

We ate venison that winter, and after I had told the story there were some mediocre jokes about "Ed's shooting gallery." But the experience seemed to work for me because I had spent a lot of time alone, moving quietly over mountains and slipping through strangled orchards, and I felt that I had earned that lucky chance, even though I had almost blown it.

It wasn't until a couple of years later, when I had studied the habits of deer, their anatomy, and had consumed some of the more prosaic literature on ballistics and the shocking power of soft-nosed bullets that it occurred to me that I probably had hit that first deer standing in the trail. And that

31

I may have hit the second one as it bolted through the cover. And that there was a good chance that one or two deer had made it over the lip of that small ravine only to bleed to death on the other side. A bonus for the foxes and crows; an oil spill on my clean, white memory of the day.

That's when I made the deal with myself. Nothing too formal, not really penitent, but the kind of loose paragraph that we add to our personal operating manual as new experiential ground is broken. So now I tend to pick a time and place to hunt that allows me to follow the deer and my own whimsy at ease, and thus I strike a good balance.

For the deer, you see, flow and trickle over the ridgetops and eskers, taking an oak bud here and bedding there, meeting and mating, shedding and dying, and all the while maintaining the communal force. And my part, now that I've set it, is to step into the current, ride it up to the ridge and try to take a piece of the flow, then find an eddy and step out.

The buck on Whitcomb Mountain is a very big piece. Heart of lion for the Masai; silver chalice for Gawain; running tide for Masefield.

Antler gleam in the morning for me.

September, 1977

Blueprint

On Thanksgiving we'll start the day earlier than most of the others. The night before we'll have set the alarm for an hour before sunrise, but one of us will awaken before it goes off, rising to the certain tick of a circadian clock that always goes duck hunting on Thanksgiving morning.

In the bedroom we'll put on turtlenecks and long underwear, wool shirts and socks, and then we'll pad quietly down to the basement, stopping to knock gently on the doors of the hunters, and taking care not to waken the rest.

We'll stop in the kitchen to put fire under the coffee pot, boil eggs and cook toast. It's a quick, and light, breakfast, but it's going to be cold out there and we'll all need the calories burning inside.

In the basement the light will be white and stark from the naked bulbs and there will be a momentary clutter of rubber and canvas, graceless torsos stumbling into awkward gear until the action sorts itself into a quieter hierarchy of those ready and those still dressing. Against the far wall the guns are neatly lined up, dark wood and worn blue, gleaming parallel in the basement light. Somebody opens a thermos, pours coffee, passes it around.

"Quarter to six. Let's go." It's the Thanksgiving shoot.

Outside the cold is a wall; wind comes hard from the north, and there are no stars. The canoes are there, tied to the old dock and resting on the marsh grass; decoys are stacked in each, paddles, and there is solid ice that breaks crinkly when someone lifts a paddle.

Each of us knows where to go. The blinds have been selected, tested and gunned during seasons past, other Thanksgivings gone by now, and the night before we will have drawn lots for them. Horse-trading will have followed, always, a kitchen clean-up assignment swapped for a spot in the pit at Two Bird Cove, or a seat in the board blind where French's Creek widens at the second big bend.

It won't really matter, though. The birds will ride the wind and play the tide, and the shooting will come as it may. Maybe it won't come at all, like the year the warm front came through on Tuesday before, and the inland ponds melted, and the birds went inland, and nobody even saw a bird all morning, and Uncle Patrick got so frustrated he stood up and threw his new Ithaca into the water in front of the blind, and he had to go back out at low tide and drag it up out of the mud.

Or maybe it will be like the year the squall line came in off the ocean, pushing squadrons of black ducks, geese, whistlers, and even the brant into the marsh, and after some of us had gotten limits we stayed and watched the action at the other blinds, cheering out loud for good dog work and hooting derision at emptied-gun misses, and Uncle Stephen had been just so damned pleased with the whole business he decided to stay in his hunting clothes all day and tried to come to Thanksgiving dinner in his waders.

Every year it's something to remember. And now it's this year, canoes slipping down the tide in the early cold of Thanksgiving morning, a lean wind coming out of the north, and dawn just a promise behind the clouded eastern sky.

Out in the marsh, we'll spread out; there will be six, maybe seven of us, a dozen decoys to put out in front of the three blinds, a few silhouettes stuck in the marsh upwind, and then we'll be ready.

Shooting light will come very slowly, and before we can see at all, there will be whistling beats in the wind above us, an early pair splashing long into the set in front of Sam and Becky. Sam will be excited, will want to jump up and take an early shot, but Becky will know better. Too dark yet, she'll say. Let them be natural decoys. And Sam will fidget, head swiveling in the growing light, wishing in the birds. They'll come.

They'll come in pairs and three's all morning long, coming low over the dunes, flaring up to survey the marsh and then banking in wide, gliding turns over one of the sets, swinging fast 20 feet in the air to turn abruptly with braking wings, feet out and stopping in midair. Bang!

They will be black ducks, mostly, and the odd bufflehead. The teal will have moved on, and it will be too early for geese, but it will be just fine with us. The black duck is right for the Thanksgiving shoot, complementary to a turkey and carefully plucked for Saturday's dinner, a somewhat rowdier affair than the quiet formality of the Thanksgiving meal itself. A duck for everyone is the goal this morning.

And by ten, we'll have succeeded or failed. Plenty of birds will have been over the decoys, and we'll have had the shots. Doug will have made a long double, his first, and won't be feeling the cold at all. Caroline might have gotten a bird, might not; sometimes we suspect she misses on purpose, but she's taken them cleanly before, and she's been hunting the longest of the four.

Back at the house, the others will have risen, made breakfast, and the hunters will gather in the kitchen over coffee and hot chocolate, milling about and already retelling the funny part, stalling over another piece of toast until plucking time. Then it will be showers, better dress, indoor manners, the holiday meal. The Thanksgiving shoot will have passed.

The Thanksgiving shoot. Not, of course, this year.

This year we've just moved from the city, and it's the first year in the house on the marsh. This year the little guys are still too young to hunt, haven't even shot a gun on their own yet. This year is the first year the families are coming to our house, the first year we haven't gone there. This year the duck season isn't even open over Thanksgiving, won't open until two weeks later.

This year is the seedling.

But I know it will grow, know what it will be. Last week I saw the promise of it.

I had been sitting on the back porch, plucking a pair of black ducks and intent on what I was doing, when I looked up to see Hope, still in her pajamas with the feet on them, standing there. I plucked a wing feather, dark on the back, white underneath, and handed it to her. She took it, smiling past the thumb in her mouth, and without saying a word went back into the house.

She didn't say a thing about it all day, but that night when we tucked her into bed, I turned just as I switched off the light. And there on her shelf among her treasures and teddy bears, lying quietly beside Bunny Rabbit and her extra special crayons, was a wing feather from a black duck, catching the last flicker of room light on an iridescent blue speculum, and flashing to me the Thanksgiving promise of all the years ahead.

November, 1978

Hiatus

You meet these people at business gatherings or parties, the sort of event where new introductions are being made and nothing gets more interesting than idle small talk. Maybe the new guy will have trout flies on his tie. Or perhaps you'll get a hint from something he says, but in any case you'll ask the question.

"Oh, you know," he'll say. "I used to hunt and fish all the time. Ever since I was a kid, you know. But now . . . I don't know. I just can't seem to find the time any more."

Then he'll shrug his shoulders a bit, and you'll probably have the good sense to change the subject. It's disappointing, and vaguely frightening, to hear him say that, to hear him admit that it's not that important to him, that he let it slip away. Don't listen to it. Turn to me instead.

Talk to me in the understated way you do when the subject is something that close to why you live. Don't overdo it, of course. Just mention in passing that you get out some yourself, that, say, you prefer a canoe, or that you like to hunt grouse with a dog. I'll get it.

I'll tell you about my days in the big covert above Goose Pond, about birds that got up in small coveys out of scrub oak in corner wood lots on Cape Cod; I'll mention my theory that the grey-phase birds are always a bit bigger than the red ones, and I might tell you about the time Whit got into porcupine quills twice in the same morning.

You may get carried away in the spirit of the moment and suggest that maybe we could get together one day and share one or two of each other's spots, your dog or mine, you'll say.

Well, I'd say, that sounds fine, but I guess we'll have to go with your dog. Whit's no kid any more, and I haven't even had him out yet this year; in fact, we only got out once last year, at that.

But I'd be happy to take you to some coverts, since I don't get down to the Cape any more, and it seems a shame to let them lie there, bull-briars and blueberries, quiet in the cold of a November afternoon, nobody to push through them with a twenty gauge. You should get to know them, let me know if the birds are still there.

Oh, sure, you'll say.

Then, if it's early in the gathering where we've met, we'll probably talk some more, and I may learn that you tie your own deer-hair, and that you think a shooting taper is just the thing for putting the bugs up under overhangs on the ponds you fish.

I'll warm up to that, and maybe I'll tell you about the running battle I've had on my own vise trying to create the fly rod version of a Rebel Popper. The closest I've come, I'll tell you, has been to whittle down some wine corks and hang fine-wire hooks on them, but the density was off and they wouldn't swim right. A couple of years ago I bought some lengths of balsa in varying diameters to experiment with, and I think that these will do the trick, but, to tell you the truth, they've been sitting in the closet and I just haven't got to it. I probably would have before now if I'd gone down to Easton for evenings in the canoe like I used to, because it would have been frustrating to be there without them, but I didn't go bass fishing at all last year.

Oh, you'll say.

Maybe I'll get to work on them this winter. June has a way of sneaking right up on you, doesn't it?

Oh yes, you'll say. June is the month for most good things. Blackflies, mostly.

And I'll chuckle at that, sharing the small thought that links us both to times past in the north country. You'll tell me about the clouds of them that you ran into up on Bog Stream last year, and that maybe you'll go up a week or two earlier this year.

Good idea, I'll agree. I hear they were worse than usual up where we go. It's probably just as well that I had to cancel out.

Neither of us will say anything for a minute or so after that, and then we'll realize that it's getting late.

Well, I guess I've got to be going, you'll say. Good luck to you. Don't take too many limits this year.

Oh no, I'll say. No, I won't do that.

I surely won't do that.

December, 1978

Peal

In late October we start to listen for the geese. Just before we go to bed, I'll go out on the porch with the dog to see if they're in yet; together we'll stand there, peering into the dark distance across the marsh and waiting for the muted *ho-onk*. If the wind is from the north, and if the birds are there, we'll hear it soon enough.

Later in the season, when the big flocks have all come down, you can hear them every night, but here in the early season, when we're waiting for the first arrivals, it's not so certain. Casey will sniff about in the dried grasses at the edge of the marsh and I'll stand there quietly, hearing only the raspy calls and feeding chuckles of the black ducks gathered on the tidal flats.

This year it followed the pattern. The night before, we'd heard nothing so Becky and I went out in the morning to the black duck blind, setting up for a pass shot or two at the birds as they headed inland to the still-open fresh water. The ducks flew early, sporadically and high, and we had no shots. Another quiet morning, it seemed, and we stood up to walk home.

Ho-onk! From the flats, just out of sight, 200 yards away. The first northern birds were in.

We knew what to do; we'd learned it the hard way the year before. Staying low, we separated; Becky moved 100 yards down the creek, Casey and I stayed put. We waited.

We waited a half hour. There was no one else on the marsh, the birds hadn't yet been shot at, and they weren't going to move until they were ready. There would be plenty of warning when they got ready.

It started with an isolated honk from one of the still-unseen birds. An answering call or two, then quiet again. A few minutes later, another honk, and a chorus of answers. There was no wind, and we could hear them loosening up, five-foot wingspans drumming the morning air, the sound coming to us like parade ground flags caught in a gusty wind. Silence again, and then they came.

They must have been working themselves into position, because they came up in a line, 150 birds fanned out across 300 yards of marsh, and they were up in a rush of pure sound.

The sound of it. We'll hear it, out on the marsh, walking in March or September; we'll come to the spot where we crouched that day and the sound will still be there, lingering in the salt air. A quick roar of wings like a breaking wave, and the honking calls all together in one long, two-toned peal, rising and spreading in front of us.

For three seconds we couldn't see them, and then they were in sight, coming over the crest of the marsh, winging easily now. Coming right at us, 200 yards away. The dog was transfixed.

I looked to the left, saw that Becky was down, ready, and that the line of geese would pass over her spot. So I put my chin on my knees and waited. The birds came on, and then they were there—fifty yards out, thirty yards up. I sat up, brought the gun to my shoulder, swung through the bird directly in front of me, and fired as the barrels blotted out his head. Nothing. I held the lead steady and shot again. The goose fell out of the air like his support string had been cut, and when the bird hit the marsh in front of me, Casey didn't need any hand signals—he was off.

I hadn't heard Becky shoot, and I turned that way in time to see her hurriedly ejecting spent shells. The geese were still above her, passing quickly, and then one of them faltered behind her, and fell. I pointed at it and shouted, and Becky turned in time to see it land in the grasses 100 yards away.

It was a great moment. The first geese of the year, Becky's first goose ever, and Casey's introduction to the art of retrieving a ten pound gamebird. My memory of it is continuous and very clear, but I have stop-action images in my mind: Becky standing on the marsh after watching the bird go down, pointing to herself and silently saying, "Me?"; the dog trying to get a grip on the goose, whining a bit in frustration and finally taking a tenuous hold of a wing near the shoulder and dragging it fifty yards to where I waited; and overlaying it all the slowly diminishing, steady calling of the geese as they faded into the brightening east sky.

It's not always that way, of course. Not even close. We try to get out every day in the season, but we rarely have the place to ourselves, especially in the late season when the big birds are out there every morning. The marsh is big, and the geese always take off into the wind—unless there's a bit of east in it, they won't come our way. And after they've heard the guns a few times they learn to take some altitude before they cross the marsh, and they leave the flats earlier every day so that by late in the season there aren't many of them around in the daylight. We call it a good season if we take a half dozen.

Black ducks are the mainstay of our season on the marsh. They're there more often, trading in and out of the marsh all day, and the shooting is usually over decoys. It's something to see them circle carefully and then commit with cupped wings, seventy yards out and coming into the set, and the dog work can be spectacular on a good day.

But when we look back across the season, feet up and lounging in a warm place, counting the days until next opening day, it's the geese that lead the parade of memories. I'm not really sure why this is.

It may be that a goose is big game, a true trophy of waterfowling. It may be the grace of the bird itself, or it may be the rarity of actually hitting one. As Reed says, when he shoots he expects a duck to fall, he's surprised when a grouse comes down, but a goose—a goose is a miracle. Probably it's all of these things, but at the top of my list is what I hear when I close my eyes.

I hear the sudden call of a single goose, coming clearly to me from an unseen place on a cold morning in November. Like a single chime from the clock tower it marks the beginning of a long afternoon, pointing toward darkness but promising much ringing before sunset.

November, 1979

Territory

There were only two cars at the landing, an old Jeep and a newer foreign compact. The Jeep had an empty boat trailer hitched to it and the compact had a padded roof rack. Across the lake, green glinting in the morning sun, the boat from the trailer trolled the spruce and granite shoreline; there were two men in the boat, one at the outboard and the other up forward. You couldn't make out the rods.

"Well, there's one of them," said John. "At least *they're* not in the river."

I just nodded my head, thinking about what might have come off the cartop rig. If it was a small canoe like ours, we'd be in trouble. Maybe.

The little river came into the lake up at the north end. Just a seepage, really, quietly spreading into the lake through the alders there, and unless you thought about it you wouldn't know the river lurked just behind the thicket. But we knew it. That's where we were going.

We knew the river was there before we ever saw it. The map said so, and if you went way down to the south end of the lake and looked up you could see the humped edges of its valley as the flow crept around Spy Mountain. In June we had decided to have a look.

The alders turned out to be a real barrier. If you paddled over to either side, you could beach the canoe, get out with some gear and bushwhack about a mile around the boggy stuff to get there. We decided against it. Instead we tried to poke the canoe through the alders themselves. It worked, sort of.

Ultimately we got through, but not until we had de-canoed a few times to drag the outfit over deadfalls and to pull through a mess of what the pros call "biotic soup." In the end it took about as long as it would have had we walked around, but this way we ended up with the canoe there. And that saved the day.

It saved the day because the river isn't wadable. The alders do retreat to the banks, but the bottom stays silty and the banks are only ten yards apart: the only reasonable way to fish it is to cast straight upstream from the middle, and to do that you've got to float. That's what we did.

At first I paddled and John cast. The casts weren't much—just daps a few yards in front of the canoe—but the fish were there. Brook trout, hordes of wild little ones. That's what we had expected.

Now it will be a long time before you catch either of us saying that a mess of wild brook trout isn't worth the effort it takes to get to them, but . . . this had been an effort. I'm not sure we would have gone back if John hadn't seen the swirl.

"Beavers in here, huh?" he said,

"Naa . . . I don't think so," I answered. "Why?"

"Well, I just saw one . . . There. Again. See where he's swimming?"

I saw. I saw bulging water and inch-high wavelets pushed out and against the banks, but I didn't see what caused it.

"You sure that's a beaver?" I asked.

"No. But what else?"

The water bulged again, same place. Neither of us said anything. I reached down with the paddle to hold the canoe in place by touching the bottom, but it was too deep. "It's deep here," I said quietly. The water moved again.

John turned back to me. "It's a fish," he said, "I saw a fin." He turned back to look at the water, then turned back to me again.

"I think it's *Jaws*," he said.

"Cast," I said.

It's not easy keeping a place like that a secret. John said that we could cut off the head and all the fins and serve the fish to unsuspecting guests as broiled lake trout. But I could just see some beady-eyed guy like Ted flipping his portion over and scanning for red and blue spots. Or I could hear

44

John's kid saying, the next time Larry came over to talk fishing. "You should have seen the huge trout daddy brought back from Spy Pond last week!"

In the end, John put it back. Put back into the water the brook trout that, if you had put it on a balancing scale, might have pushed a five-pound bag of sugar toward the ceiling. Instead, it pushed a vee-wake for thirty yards upstream before vanishing in the rich, red-brown water. For a very long time we sat there, watching.

Now we were back. We waited until the trollers were far down the lake, and then we scuttled the canoe quickly to the alders and poked into an opening. When we got to the first carry-over we stopped and were about to get out for the chore when we saw the other canoe. It was coming out. There was one man in it, an older guy, and when he got to his side of the deadfall, he stopped and looked at us.

"You fellers lost?" he asked. You could tell he knew better.

"No. You?" That was stupid: he was on the way *out*.

"Been here before," he answered. "You?"

"Been here before."

"Well," he said. His face hadn't changed.

"We'll give you a hand," John said. "There's two of us." The other guy was still for a second, then nodded his head once, sharply.

His canoe was old, too. A cedar-strip Rushton-type, I guessed that he'd made it himself, but I didn't ask. When we lifted it, we saw the trout laid out on the ribs; there were three of them, 18 or 20 inches apiece.

"Nice fish," said John.

"How'd you fellers find this place?" the man asked.

"Just found it," answered John.

"All by yourselves? You just came up here?"

"Yeah, that's right," said John.

The older man was quiet then as we got his canoe settled and started to work ours over the deadfall.

"You tell anyone about it?" he asked.

"Never do that," said John, looking right at him. The old man looked back for a minute and then started to paddle out. As he paddled away he said something that we couldn't hear.

"How's that?" called John, but the little Rushton just slipped away. John looked over at me, and I shook my head. We went fishing.

I'm pretty sure the old man never came back.

February, 1981

Vows

The black flies weren't supposed to be there yet; it was only Memorial Day.

When we got to the put-in place, the sandy ridge above the lake where we always park the car between two white pines, you couldn't yet tell that the bugs were already out. The wind off the water was strong in our faces and we hurried to unload—canoe, paddles and a true excess of gear for just three days on the lake. Hope and Sam were with us this time.

It's about two miles from the car to the campsite we like: a beach exposed ten years ago when the old dam went out. Upwind today, and just three hours of daylight remaining. With a seven- and a four-year-old aboard, and with enough gear to bring us down to eight inches of freeboard on the big Old Town, we were beaten before we shoved off.

. Except that we didn't know it yet, Becky and I both wanted the good camp, so we tried for it. For about 25 minutes we tried to push our way up the lake. It's a long, narrow and spruce-edged Maine "pond" and when the wind is from the northwest it has a bit more than five miles of open water in which to build waves. At our end these were three-foot whitecaps. We weren't having any fun.

So I yelled at Becky in the bow and said that we should head to the west shore and look for a beach. The kids just sat there huddled, backs to the spray with mouths closed and eyes wide.

I knew that there were a couple of small islands over there, just an acre or two each and lying just 100 yards or so from the shore, so I angled the canoe in that direction and like a migrating bird we kept pushing ahead while the wind set us over in the direction we really wanted to go. In a couple of minutes we were in the lee.

It's one of the great moments in canoeing, slipping in behind a rocky shelf and having the ceaseless pressure of the wind vanish instantly. The canoe comes alive again and glides ahead in proper proportion to your paddle's effort, and it only takes a minute of this change to replace depression with euphoria.

We had arrived. An island to call our own for three days. Logistics and planning left my mind; I wanted to fish.

The canoe was quickly beached and we all got out to fish. Light spinning rods—closed-face for Sam—and Rebels and Rapalas; downwind for now. Nothing. It was time to pitch camp.

The shore of the island had no beaches as such. All the level spots were rocky. So we went into the trees, and right away we found a beauty: about ten feet above the water and 20 yards back in under the spruces. There was plenty of room for the tent and a cooking area. And no bugs. Just as we had figured. No place to be in mid-June, though, we said.

The tent and the Sims stove went up quickly, and the kids arranged bags and duffle, and then we had time to explore around the perimeter of our island. It was bassy-looking water, but we raised no fish. We liked the look of the place, though, and as it got on toward evening the wind faded away. A hermit thrush sang to us and a loon called from away across the water. I felt the city and the planning, the long drive and the need to answer to other people all slide out of me. Three more days. A gift.

That night, as we cooked dinner, there were a few mosquitoes. Strange, we said, that they'd be out ahead of the black flies. The kids didn't like being bitten while trying to eat, and they disappeared into the tent. Within half an hour we were in there with them.

When we woke in the morning, it was warm, windless and sunny. And the netting at the front of the tent was alive with black flies.

I wasn't very worried about this because we had plenty of Muskol and Becky and I each had Shoo-Bug jackets. If you take care with these defenses, you can handle anything entomological and bloodthirsty. So we all suited up, tucked

48

pants into socks and buttoned our shirts at the neck, doped up and stepped out.

It worked well enough for a while, but we had to move down to the shore to eat, trying to catch what little breeze there was. Hope and Sam began to complain about the bugs, so to distract them I rigged their rods. Hope could cast a short distance and liked being self-sufficient; Sam could crank back in if I cast it out for him, which I did and then turned back to get another cup of coffee. I hadn't made it to the pot before I heard Sam laughing; when I turned there was a 12-inch bass jumping at the end of his line and Sam was still cranking as if it weren't there. By the time I got back to him the fish was all the way up to the tip-top and Sam was craning him onto the beach. I slowed down and pulled out my little camera.

It's the best picture from the trip. Partly because it's a great picture, but also because there aren't many others. We didn't catch any more fish by camp that morning, and because the black flies were really getting to the kids and to Becky, we packed a quick lunch and set out in the canoe.

In the middle of the lake it was a bit better, but we couldn't get completely away from the biters. Out by the huge mid-lake boulders I began to take some smallmouths on the fly rod, and for a while I didn't notice that the kids weren't fishing at all, and that Becky wasn't doing much either. The flies had dampened them, and they were trapped; we spent the rest of the day on the water avoiding the clouds of bugs nearer shore. Toward dark we rushed to camp, made a quick dinner while the kids stayed in the tent, and then we all ate together inside the screens. Outside the loons were calling near, the sky was deepening to purple and I figured it would be a good night to hear owls. I was about to go back out to fish the shallows in the twilight, to make that nearly sacramental gesture of raising a smallmouth in the last glow of evening, when I looked over at Hope and Sam and Becky. Their eyes talked to me.

The children were beaten, worn down by the constant buzzing, stinging and welting. Another day of it was not in them. And Becky was a mother who saw this in her children, and she was hurt by it.

I teetered there for a moment, torn between their physical discomfort and my psychic need. Caught and stretched between an immovable duty and a private craving. Hung.

"Okay," I said. "We'll pack up in the morning. We'll go home."

May, 1982

Place

In the center of the spruce bog the trees lie in a jumble and it's hard to tell which of them are alive and which have given up, slowly on their way down to the mat, leaning heavily on the others.

When you walk there the mat is soft and green even in the late fall, and if there is snow there you can kick it aside and the lush green will appear underneath. If you kick a little harder, the veneer of mosses will split easily and tear, showing the rich humus underneath and showering the snow cover around the edges of your footprint like a houseplant dropped onto a white rug. At the edge of the bog, where the open hardwoods—maples mostly, some beech and yellow birch—give way to the dry ground spruces, the floor is harder and the high branches of the evergreens capture the falling snow so that there is less of it on the ground.

When you come to the bog following a buck track, you'll get your first sharp look at the tracks here in the shallow, undisturbed snow dusting the hard ground. Don't be embarrassed; take out a 30-06 round and lay it in the track just like Larry Benoit says to do. If it doesn't lie flat in the bottom, then this probably is not the biggest deer in these woods. Are you going to stop following him? Stop here and think about it.

Here. Start with "here." About half way up Burnt Mountain, looking south. Somewhere down there is the tent, stacked wood, cold stove, the jeep. Across the valley, faint now in the mid-morning grey, are the Birch Hills, with Larry and Reed somewhere on them. And you are right here, in a place you've not seen before, among trees. Trees that, had you come into this bog 50 yards to the right, you would not have seen. Ever. Take off a glove and lay your hand on one.

Now you've done it. Sealed it hard. Twenty years from now, somewhere—who knows where, you'll take off another glove and this tree, this half-grown spruce, will be with you. You'll feel it then, just as now.

How many places have you known like this? How many trees, marsh hummocks, beach pebbles, alder tangles and mountain streamlets have you sat by or stood in, all alone, lost in a kind of reverie that you are without ability to describe? How many moments like this have you had? Will have again? How many places like this bog are there for you?

Like this bog? Look into it; let your eyes follow the buck track deep into the dark of it. Like this bog? None. None at all. This place, a place without edges save those that you put there with your mind, is the only place there is right now. You made sure of that.

You made sure of it starting last summer when you spread all of the maps out on the floor and started looking for a new place. You wrote letters to paper company foresters and state forest wardens, and then you scoured all of the books ("Where To Go In Maine," "Hunter's Guide To The Northeast," "Deer Hunting Outlook"). You wrote to the Fish & Wildlife people and got last year's deer kill statistics, then you spent whole evenings trying to pick a place that had deer, good hills, rough roads and only a few hunters. You then learned (the very hard way) that the Soil Conservation Service had consolidated its aerial photography office with the Geological Survey and several others and had moved to Salt Lake City to a building that has a six-line mailing address. Eight weeks later you got the aerial photographs; it was 22 days before deer season.

So you told Larry and Reed that you had a new place, but maybe, just maybe, we ought to go in there a couple of days early to take a look.

There was new snow in that high country, and after ten miles the old logging road was a white carpet—no jeep tracks at all. The country was yours. It took all of the rest of the day to make a good camp: firewood for a week, a four-square job of setting the big tent, a layer of sand and dirt in the sheetmetal stove. And all the day you stole glances up, up at Burnt Mountain, fading hardwood-to-spruce and out of sight in the snowmist of November. In the morning you'd go up there.

At dawn you started, slowly this first time on the new mountain, checking the compass often, and by eight you had the buck track, traversing and quartering uphill, moving northeast. You moved with him, scope caps off now, and two hours later he brought you to the bog.

The tracks went in.

And here you are. A shiny 30-06 round on the ground. Your ungloved hand resting on a spruce trunk. Breakfast a memory, lunch in your pocket, dinner four miles of unbroken trees away. This is it, precisely. This is not, you know, a trophy buck. This is a trophy place.

Turning after the tracks, you go in.

October, 1982

Bearing Away

Lately I've been thinking about the Madison River. You know what it's like—maybe you've been on it. Rich water, big country: the definition of Paradise for some of the more serious fishermen I know.

I've never seen it.

Well, that's not quite true. When I was seven my parents took my brothers and me to Yellowstone, so I probably saw it on that trip, but I'm talking about "seeing," not "looking at."

Anyway, what I've been thinking about the Madison is this:

It's a river of attributes, and high on that list is the fact that you know what it is. Where it is. What swims in it. And, if you read a bit, who fishes it when, and with what success. You know these things, or most of them, because the Madison is . . .

Here's where I've been getting bogged a bit down.

I know that you can go there, and that you can fish in the beauty of Yellowstone, or farther downstream in the big water of the west side. You can cast dry flies in long glides or toss muddlers on stiff leaders to wild spawning brown trout in the fall. In the spring there will be broods of Canada geese and the singing of thrush in the aspens, and as the season passes, you will share the beaver meadows with elk and moose and river otters and you will stand thigh-deep in the moving heart of preserved wild fishing in America.

But I also know this: It's a place without secrets.

Go to a Trout Unlimited or Federation of Fly Fishermen meeting and someone will say, drink in his hand, after the introduction by your friend Fred, "When were you last on the Madison?"

54

"Actually, I've never fished it . . ."

A blank look. Then, "Well, man, you want to catch some fish . . . Tell you what, you get yourself to Bud Lilly's and then . . ."

Or, easier yet, go to the books and magazines and look for it. It'll be there, flowing smooth blue out of the Firehole and across the pages. There will be fly casters there and they will be happy to tell you when to fish, and how. And why. And . . . and they will be right. They'll even be right about the "why." For the river is for real; just look at it.

As the man said: it just don't get any better than this. And it's there for all and each of us, whenever we want it.

You ought to do it. I ought to do it, and I will.

In fact, the only reason that I haven't been there is that these other little places keep getting in the way. Places that you don't know much about.

One of them is a small rock. Worn granite, I think. Up north. You can sit on it with your wader feet in the current and around behind you from the left comes a feeder brook.

If you sit there, the first you'll notice is the water sound—trill, trill, trill-a and the occasional gurgle—and a bit later you'd realize that there is a wind-rustle in the maples and chickadees in the alders. Nothing new there; I'm sure you'd notice it right away, picking it all out from experience and times alone in other places.

But if you were, for a minute, me there would be something else. A part of you would be slipping upstream in the feeder, past the first rundown beaver dams and around the spruce hillocks to the open hardwoods where the stream runs roundabout for two miles and then ends—starts, really—in the seepage emanating from the slip-slide jumble of the rock-wall that marks the true beginning of Number Three Mountain.

The true beginning of Number Three Mountain. And the beginning of other things, too, not so easily marked. Just over to the east (hard to measure distance, here in the deep woods, in the leaf-cover of fishing time) is where the moose bed down in November, uphill from where you saw the bear track last year, and a good distance to the west of where you had been three years before when you thought that the road should have been near but it wasn't and you kept moving on a compass line, very much in doubt for the last 20 minutes, and moving, moving south until there it was and then you could actually feel the woods rotating around you as your mind reset itself to the very plain reality of a road running exactly 90 degrees different than you had thought it would be just the minute before.

The little brook that now cools your feet could take you there quickly, and you know it now as you sit. And you know other things—that the brook flows down to camp, to a tent sitting on the bared spot where it has come and gone six seasons now. There are markers there. Oaken tent pegs broken off deep in the dirt in cold seasons, and rock-dams in the spring flowage where beer cooled in other Junes. And voices, loud with today and fading muted from before. Sitting here now, on the rock—it is granite, it's so quiet—you can strain to reach forward for the voices to come. Hear them? Hear them? No . . .

No, I can't hear them, either. Not now. That will come when they come. For now, I'll stay here, in this brook, downstream from before, upcurrent from what's next. I'm going to tie on a dry fly, and I'm going to cast it up to before and watch it drift to the future. Maybe a little brook trout will dismantle this piece of time in its passage.

And all the while, and later at night in the tent, white pine whisper overhead, I'll wonder about this: Can you have this on the Madison River? Does it work so neatly as it does in the unknown places, or does your Number Six Goofus Bug time machine collide with the bumpy passage of other memories, other's memories, plans?

I don't know.

February, 1983

Futures

When I gave Douglas his first fly rod this year we spent the better part of Saturday morning rigging it up. You only get one first fly rod, and you only get to give one to each child. It was a moment for both of us.

First out of the box was the rod itself, and I let Douglas put the two pieces together right away, right there in the living room. For an 11-year-old he's got careful hands; nobody got a tip-top in the eye and the rod survived a couple of minor ceiling scrapes. You can drive a guy buggy with too many "watch out's."

I got Douglas the youth's outfit from the L. L. Bean catalog. I couldn't have done much better by picking components, and their set-up comes with the new Dave Whitlock handbook, a good one. Besides, I wanted it all to arrive in one box, like mine had.

It came in March, a couple of weeks late for the birthday, but a fine time to get a new fishing rod. In our country, a good two months ahead of topwater time. Plenty of time for practice.

But before you can practice, you've got to rig up, so we got to it right after breakfast on Saturday.

Now there are lots of shortcuts in fishing, and for me most of them make sense. Techniques and pre-defined accomplishments are not things that I care much for in my fishing and the shortest distance between being home and not fishing and being on the water tricking fish is the route I want. With exceptions, of course.

One of the exceptions I learned the very hard way is that you *do* put backing on the reel, and that you *do* smooth out the splice with epoxy. Remembering the instant slack at my end of the strung-out line as the leader popped at the other end as the fish (Who knows—I never saw it) vanished downstream, I asked Doug to turn to the knot-tying part of the Whitlock book. That's all. No lectures, no "I remember the time . . ." Just a quiet insistence that we put some backing on the reel, that we smooth-epoxy the knot, and that we think of something else to do for a few hours while the glue dried.

It drove him crazy, I know.

And when it dried, we cranked the fly line onto the reel, and then I nail-knotted a bit of .023 monofilament to the end and tied a quick surgeon's knot loop on the other end. A matching loop on the leader and there it was. I showed Doug how the two loops mate to attach the leader. He thought it was neat. I thought of the number of times that his fly was going to catch in that snare as he cast in days—years—to come. How his loops would finally have enough arc in them to get past on his false casts only to snag again as he pushed too hard on the release. How many bluegills were going to ignore his fly and snap at the loops instead.

I didn't say a word.

Outside on the grass I showed him how to string up by pushing the fly line through and letting the leader trail behind. I figured that he didn't have to learn *everything* himself, and I wanted to minimize his aggravations to those that might teach him something about the fishing itself. I never once mentioned wind knots. He's on his own there—Whitlock talks about them in the book.

After a very brief demonstration with the hookless set up, I gave the rod to Doug and let him have a go at it.

He was better after ten minutes than I had been after a few days, and he stayed with it till dark. By May he's going to be just fine at frontlawn fly casting.

And then we're going fishing, right about the time the lilacs are prime. I'll put him in the bow seat of the canoe and I'll paddle him around the pond for a few hours, trying to keep the wind on his left shoulder. I'm going to take him to a pond that he doesn't know well and I'll steer him over the bluegills and black crappies until he develops a little hook-setting timing. If he gets it, then he's going to find himself a short cast away from an old dock piling and I'm going to bet him that he can't cast his fly anywhere near it.

You and I know what will happen if he does get near it; I'm not sure that Doug does, but I'm hoping it works.

Because if it does, if he does get that good explosion under his fly, then I'm going to turn him loose. After that he'll be pretty much on his own. At least for most of the time. Because after that he'll be hooked, and then he's just got to build time, experience and preference.

Because someday Douglas is going to be out there, talking tactics with another fisherman, and when he decides what he prefers I hope that he doesn't start the explanation with, "My Dad always says . . ."

No. What I want to hear is something like, "What I've learned is . . ."

Because, you see, I expect to be that other fisherman, standing next to him, learning something from a good fly caster.

I'll let you know how it turns out.

April, 1983

Intent

For three years, until a couple of years ago, we lived in a house on an island in the middle of a salt marsh. The house was about ten years old and had lots of big windows; from nearly every room you could stand and stare at the marsh. That's what I did.

For three years I watched the small and big action on the grasses and mud, followed the yellowlegs and foxes, listened to the fish crows and the Canada geese, saw the seasons slip and come. I learned to anticipate the tides, and I found the deer trails.

I spent hours walking the marsh, in and out of hunting season, with and without the dog. And for every hour I spent out on it, I know that there were ten or twenty spent at the windows, just staring.

After a few months of this, I started seeing things more clearly, and more often. I'd come home in the late afternoon, walk down to the big windows in the living room, and take a look. Something would catch my eye right away; something in a tree on the far side of the marsh, a little over a mile away. A long minute of careful staring yielded nothing more: something in a tree on the far side of the marsh.

The ten-power Zeiss's would solve it: red-tail in an oak tree.

Other times—most times—the scene before me would lie quiet in its familiarity. Gentle winds and lapping waves, sea-gulls banking easy and the pastel shift of spartina greens and brown. It would calm me like oncoming sleep.

Until something moved. My eyes would be on it before my mind knew that something had happened, just as your hand retracts from the flame before you know your finger is cooking.

Usually it was nothing exciting. A seagull coming up out of a tidal creek or a fish crow hopping off a piece of driftwood. Some times I never would detect what it was that had caught my attention; I'd look and look and look again.

Those unseen attention-getters were what lasted, for I never doubted that I had in fact seen something. No figments allowed. It—whatever—had been there for an instant in my periphery, and was gone. What was it?

And the unknown memory of it would linger, nagging, even as I looked on across the expanse. My eyes would come back to the spot even as my mind moved away; my mind would stay on it as my eyes shifted away. A sea anchor.

New things on the marsh didn't always present themselves at first sight. This was especially true of the birds; it might take a full 30 seconds of relaxed scanning before a blue heron, hanging still and angular over a pothole, would resolve itself. A hawk could get halfway across in flight before its different wingbeat would separate it from the gulls. A duck, on the other hand . . .

A duck I'd pick out as I saw it, no later. I wanted ducks.

But what were most jarring when they presented themselves were deer. Deer I'd see once or twice a week, pretty much all year long, more so in the spring and fall. I looked for them always, wanting to see them, and a flush of contentment would come over me when one would appear, slipping out of the woods at the edge and walking easily. Red in the summer, grey in the fall, I could tell the fawns from the yearlings, the yearlings from the adults, and after not too much time I could easily tell a buck even with dropped antlers. Swaggering male chauvinism is alive and well among whitetails.

A deer along the edge I wouldn't see until it moved. Tree trunks and thick shrubs don't move laterally, so when something that size slipped along the edge it presented itself immediately.

I'm sure that none of these animals or birds knew that I watched them from the windows; none was aware that I was there. And I'm just as certain that none of them tried to get too close to the house without being seen—at least not in the daytime.

It's interesting to imagine it. Would I see one if it tried? Really tried. I just don't know.

I do, however, know this: If you moved into that house on the marsh tomorrow and started looking out one of the windows, and if I happened to be standing in the middle of the marsh when you did, I could probably get down out of sight and off the marsh and into the trees without your ever knowing I was there. It would take me a long time, and it would be a messy sneak, but if it meant enough to me, I could do it.

A month or two later, after you had learned the marsh, the shape of the land and its ragged edges, and knew what should move where, you'd see me before I could get down, or you'd catch me on the lurk.

You see, it's not that hard to be fooled, even when you're paying close attention. You didn't notice, for instance, that for the last couple of minutes you've been reading a genuine hook-and-bullet "how to" article.

Did you?

August, 1983

Question

It will take nine or ten hours to get there, and after the first eight hours the trip will only be half over. That's because only those last two hours will be on the dirt road. And I always figured that one hour on the rough was equal to four on the smooth.

I like the rough.

It will be a lot farther north than the old camp, and although none of us has seen that country, I've already got a pretty fair picture of it in my mind.

It's a land of rocky streams running through low hills, and the loggers are active there. They cut our section sometime in the Fifties and they let the slow-growing hardwoods re-seed naturally. Lately that hasn't happened; the foresters have become less patient and now they put down herbicides after a cut and replace only spruce and fir because the soft-woods grow faster. This is not a good thing for the deer and the grouse. And it's not a good thing for my kids, who will have to look hard for a good stand of hardwoods in which to teach their children how to hunt deer in the big woods.

But for now, and for some years to come, the good places are still there. You can find them just by looking at the map. Looking hard and with purpose, that is.

Our purpose is to get back in the country so that we can hunt alone—away from other people and away from each other—all day long. This is not easy to find. Already Larry has spent three days scouting one place that looked good. It looked good, that is, until he chanced a conversation in a diner 30 miles away and found out that the country looked good to the local boys, too. Day hunters. Did okay up there, too, they said.

So we're going north, and then we're going in on the dirt,

over the rocks and across a couple of streams. We'll stay a week, like we always do.

I can see it now, driving in. The mind-flattening hum of 300 miles of macadam switched off as we make the first turn onto the logging road. It's always flat ground, that first mile or two into the woods, and before the Jeep gets to the first real pitch, I'll be hunting.

Not road-hunting, that is. Not actually looking for a deer yet. But reading the country. And, yes, wanting to see game. After all, we worked hard to select and find this place and it would be rewarding to see it rich in the things that are supposed to live here.

So I study the country hard as we drive through it. And slowly, slowly as the chimera and quick-flashing gestalts form themselves in the passing, I begin the descent into the question.

Okay, now . . .

The question has a preamble; it lies rooted in the fact that only once in all the hunts has any one of us shot a deer before the last day or two of the hunt. Our purpose is therefore untested; we've had to hunt hard, dawn to dusk every day, and we've had to go back into the thick stuff and onto the high ridges and across the dim basins, always looking. Always looking.

As the ad says, we've done it the old-fashioned way . . .

One time, in the old place, Larry found a good track under the rock slide and followed it all the way back to where the buck crossed the road 200 yards from camp.

The question . . .

The animal must have, he figured, gone by in mid-morning, close enough to stop and sniff at the lingering cookstove smoke.

What if . . .

In fact, Larry could see where the buck did just that, the tracks turning a bit just the far side of the road.

A man could set up . . .

In the old camps this was a rare thing; we had to get some distance from the tent to get to game, and this has always been fine with us. You need the pre-light hike to get going and, after all, this is a hunt, not a shoot.

Yes, but what if . . .

We take care selecting our campsites, seeking not to place the little compound of tents in the middle of the cover. Water and centrality are the keys and when the location is found we'll spend a whole day setting up. Most of the time is consumed in getting firewood—scouting for standing dead cedar and maple; cutting, hauling, splitting, stacking.

Maybe one of us should bring a rifle along, in case . . .

Then, after camp is rigged and if there still is some light, we may get in the now-empty Jeep and cruise up the road a ways, looking for good entry-points into the woods so they'll be easier to find in the dark of the morning.

What if a good buck should . . .

Then we'll drive back to camp for the first night in the bags, and if the hunt follows form, the Jeep will stay cold and unstarted for the week. We came for the silence, and what we don't want is internal combustion breaking it up.

Yes, but didn't you really come to get a deer . . .

One year I hunted hard for six days and never saw a deer. Two days later, at home, walking the driveway along the marsh, I came face-to-face with an eight-point buck, rigid in the scrub oak and arrowroot and staring at me from 15 feet.

Exactly. So what will you do if it happens in the new camp, the first day, while you're still setting up?

Well . . . I guess I won't worry about it. It's pretty unlikely.

Wrong. You keep going into that country, going way back in on rough roads, and it's going to happen.

Well . . . we came for the hunt. For the richness of the wilderness experience. I'd let him . . .

Are you sure?

. . .

Are you sure?

No, I guess . . .

Well?

No, I'm not sure.

October, 1983

Primer

The kids were playing in the other room, and they had some friends over. I was sort of tuned out, but I picked it up in the middle . . .

"Yes it is . . ."

"Naah."

"Yes, *sir* . . ."

"Yeah, sure."

"Hey, Dad. Isn't that so?"

I was in it now. "Is what so?"

"A baby eagle is bigger than its mom."

Hmmm. The right answer, filled with caution and hedges, or the quick one?

"Well, not at first. But later, like the one we saw, it's bigger until it learns to fly a lot and it can burn off the baby fat . . ."

"See? I told ya . . ."

". . . yeah, and it was *close*."

"How close?"

"About to that tree out there."

"Geez . . ."

Quiet again, except for the usual odd noises. Paper rustling, small rubber wheels on carpet, nose sniffles.

"And Caroline saw a bear."

"No way."

"Yeah really. With Dad. It was across the lake running. We were in the tent. They saw it with the binoc's."

Reflection in the other room.

"Can bears swim?"

"*I* don't know . . . Hey, Dad. Can bears swim?"

You have to love the direct here-to-there of a kid's mind. *Jaws IV* with fur.

"Sure can." I figured I'd let it sit. *Jaws IV* with wet fur.
"Did you see the bear again?"
"Oh, no. They like to hide. Dad says they're shy."
"Oh."
"Anyway, it was really far away."
"Oh."
"Way across the lake."
"Yeah."
Back to the mumbled action . . .
"What else?"
"Lots."
"Like what."
"Well, we camped out every night. With a fire and stuff.
Right on the beach."
"Neat."
"Yeah. And you could hear loons."
"Loons?"
"Yeah, *you* know, like my mom's decoy over there. We saw
a mom with babies swimming."
"Oh, you could hear them swimming?"
"*No*-oo, dummy. They make weird noises. Like . . ."
Loon calls (sort of) in the living room, in February. Boy
George, meet your betters.
All this while the regular tempo of play went on: a new
assault by G.I. Joe, a quick fashion change for Barbie, some
obscure scuffle with the cat. And holding over it all, the
looming imagery of the north woods. Loons, black bears,
ospreys, wild blueberries, woodsmoke at breakfast and pat-
tering rain on nylon in the night. Once again I let it fade into
background noise. A nice feeling . . .

"Hey, Dad."
"What."
"Was that a fishing trip, or a camping trip?"
Hmmm . . .
"I don't know, guys. What do you think?"
". . . a fishing trip, 'cause I caught . . ."
". . . both . . ."
". . . a *canoe* trip."
"Well, I guess it was all of those, huh?"

General agreement signified by a chorus of "yeah's."
Play noises again; not much talk. "Hey, Dad."
"Yep."
"We're going again this year, aren't we?"

Contentment is delivered in so many ways, isn't it?

February, 1984

Singular

Two guys were standing ahead of me in the line. Outdoor clothes, worn boots, faces unshaven on a Friday night. Here's the story as I heard it:

". . . so now the guy figures he's finally found the main stream, even if he is on the wrong side of it. End of panic.

"He starts heading downstream. That's what you do—right?—when you're lost in the big woods, and pretty soon the stream's getting wider and the guy is starting to relax 'cause really he's only been gone a few hours, and Bam! he comes around a bend and there's the Boy Scouts."

"The *Boy* Scouts?"

"Well . . . I don't know. Some bunch of kids. Campers. Whatever. Anyway he saw 'em and that was it."

"*It?*"

"Yeah. He went back upstream. He went fishing, like he was supposed to."

"Oh."

Oh. That's what I said. That's, in fact, what I felt. There it was—a metaphor for upscale outdoor practice delivered as a freebie right there in the check-out line at L. L. Bean. It was a long line and I had some time to think it over.

Let's see. The river as mother-metaphor. Okay. Who can quibble?

When in doubt, move downstream till you see something to regain your confidence, then get back up. Sounds good.

Stay away from, i.e., above, the unlearned mob on the lower stretches. Right.

And when you do get it all back together, go fishing. Hey . . .

So, oh newly-learned one in the check-out line, how does it all help with the weekend plan?

Well . . .

Well, the pre-enlightenment plan was to drive up as close to the good water as the Jeep could handle, hike in with the tent and a set of waders and fish for three days within a walk of the campsight. Alone.

Alone.

That was the new part, the variation on the old theme. And it had cost some to obtain . . .

"You want to go up there *alone*? To a new river in a part of the country where you've never been, and you're going *alone*?

"Uh huh."

"But . . ."

"It's okay. It's just something I want to do."

"Fine. But . . ."

"It's in the middle of the black flies."

". . ."

"And our trip wasn't until August anyway."

". ."

"We're definitely going. This is extra."

". "

And there I definitely was, three hours north of the house, standing in the L. L. Bean line, on my solo trip. One more gas stop and then nothing but the silence. One hand clapping, and all that.

Who was that guy? I wondered. The lost-and-found guy. Me? Naah. I'm still in line, and I don't get lost anyway; I've done my homework on this one. I know the country well, even though I've never been exactly there.

The river is a stream up there, worn granite and brook trout, beaver dams that the paper companies leave alone because no road is near, moose around the bogs. Plenty of spruce and no budworm damage yet—the loggers are busy elsewhere. I really wanted to go there alone.

I wanted to be alone for the same reasons you like to be alone somewhere, and for maybe a couple more. Depends on how hard you've thought about it.

On most of my trips, with John and Larry or Reed, or with

Becky or the kids, or some combination, there is an undercurrent of banter, of tales and comments. It's expected, and there is a pattern. The stories are about the other trips, of course; those are the finished ones and the editing is complete. But the effect is this: while we are doing one thing, we're thinking about another. That has its plusses, of course, blending and knitting the times into a sort-of tapestry, but it's got to detract some from the moment at hand.

I read somewhere—I think it was in *The Complete Wilderness Paddler*—that every time you use a camera on a trip you cease being on the trip itself and instead have placed yourself in the future, looking back at the recorded images of the time. That's what the camera's for, right?

Well, I wanted to cut out both those detractions. I wanted to go alone, and to go in a way that would require my concentration. I wanted to pay attention to the getting there; I wanted to pay attention to the living there; I wanted to pay attention to the fishing there. And then I wanted to pack up and go home. I wanted to be about as talkative as a cow moose.

And I was on my way to the doing of it. Well on my way, that is, until the dissertation in the L. L. Bean line . . .

. . . at which point I got a second thought. More of a flash, actually. It was me up there, bug-bitten, stumbling into the Boy Scouts . . .

But, no. Not me. Never happen.

. . . oh, yeah. What about . . .

I *said* no. It'll never happen.

. . . but it has . . .

No. This is a good thing, and I've planned it out. This is the real thing.

Look. Let me ask you this:

Have you ever had a truly simple fishing trip?

May, 1984

71

Free Fall

You always see them in the spring and summer, usually in pairs but often enough in ragged strings above the lakes and bogs of fishing time.

The summer geese and ducks are an increment, an expected decoration for the long days and cool twilights of the north country in full bloom. You'll be paddling around a bend at the inlet to Musquadabook Lake, easing into the flat water and pickerel grass and reaching for your rigged fly rod, when three mergansers come zipping by, ten feet off the water and cruising.

Or maybe you'll be sitting at the morning fire, a high overcast softening the light as the woodsmoke slips straight up and someone else is doing the breakfast clean-up. You've just finished your second cup of coffee and as you start to get up to help you see them. Black ducks, you figure, but maybe mallards; seven—no, eight—of them across the lake and above the spruces, heading south.

Heading south.

But no, you say, it's just chance. they're not leaving yet. Not in August . . .

Sure. Don't worry. It's still fishing . . .

Yeah, right. Fishing.

But . . .

But what?

But the teal have already left.

The teal have. . . No, I saw some yesterday. Greenwings.

Oh, some are still here. They haven't all left.

Yeah.

. . .

What?

Seen any bluewings?

This year, up on the lake in August, the fishing really is excellent. A wet year has kept the streams high and the water temperature down; trout are active in the streams and bass are still on top, looking for poppers. You don't have to fight the mosquitos at twilight just to get in a little surface action, and today is a bonus: clouds to keep the sun off the water.

So it's the long paddle to the rocks and bars at the end of the lake, a day trip that you don't make every year, waiting for a year like this and a day to match so that the time spent in transit down there and back to camp will pay off. You don't even want to think about a headwind.

And there is none now, none likely later. At the end of the lake, an hour after breakfast, you find that the fish have moved away from the rocks and are moving in the weeds and pads of shallow water.

Move in with them.

And watch in gaping stupor as thirty geese get up honking a hundred yards in front of the canoe. It takes them a full two minutes to get out of sight over Firetower Hill to the west.

Did you see that?

Did I *see* it?

Geese. There are geese up here.

Yeah, I know.

Well . .

Well, they weren't heading south.

Not yet, you mean.

Look . . .

Okay, okay.

A mid-morning lull in the fishing, still in the shallows, down lake. You put down the fly rod and reach for the old ammo can to get at the binoculars.

Looking for more geese?

No. Just looking.

Mmmm . . .

I am. Just looking.

Right.

Blue heron over there . . .

You know you . . .

. . . fishing.

. . . can . . .

What? What now?

All I was saying was that you can use that ammo can for ammo, you know.

I know. I do. At home on the duck hunts. You know that.

Yeah.

And a bit later, after the heron moves off and all the other grey possibilities are resolved into the stumps and hillocks of reality, you put down the binoculars, reach again for the fly rod.

Some people do do it, you know.

Do what?

Hunt this country.

Of course they do.

For ducks.

Yeah.

And geese.

I know. But they're locals . . .

You could do it, you know . .

I know.

You could do it just like you are now. A couple of canoes. Bring the wall tent and the dog. Decoys. Set up for three or four days and work the marshy edges . . .

I do know . . .

Sure you do.

I do. I've always thought about it. It's been in my mind since Kenny first came up here and saw the marshes and the birds. I think about it a lot on the long drive up and back every year. It's a good thing. I'll do it.

This year?

I don't know.

. . .

Well, I don't. It's tough getting the time.

. . .

It *is*. And it's no sure thing, you know. I don't know when the birds pack up out of here. I don't know when the lakes ice up.

. . .
Well, it's true
. . .
What?
. . .
C'mon. What?
How old are you?

August, 1984

A Song for Norbert

Maybe you knew him; he had a lot of friends. From the day that we met him in 1976 until the night last week when he left us, all of us here depended on Norb Buchmayr, relied on him, trusted him . . . and loved him. And for all of that, we always got more back from Norb than we could give him. Now he's made sure that it will forever remain so.

It seems that the invitations always came from Norb. "C'mon up," he'd say. "I've taken care of it."

"But . . ."

"Don't wor-ry. I'll han-dle it."

He always handled it; we always went. To the Vermont uplands in October, to some over-stuffed reception in a hotel in Atlanta, to the nighttime surf on Nantucket. It didn't matter, not if the situation was in Norb's hands. It didn't matter, because Norb's were the hands that did most things the way they were meant to be done, whether it was swinging his Browning, dialing his telephone or—at the top of his list—tousling a red-headed kid's hair. Good hands. Count it as a privilege if you ever shook one of them.

As you read this, had things been different, I'd have been once again on a beach on Nantucket with Norb and a few others lucky enough to call him a friend. When he called in April to talk about it, I got, as usual, excited about the prospect, so I sat down and wrote a little piece about Norb's annual Nantucket trip. I was going to print it here without telling him, hoping he'd smile a bit when he read it. Well . . .

Well, Norb, here it is. More than ever, it's for you.

West tide, east wind. Dark night. That's what you want in June on Nantucket Island.

You don't always get them, of course. Not out on the long sand where starlight alone can guide your booted feet over rutted jeep tracks until you can walk easily in the wave flattened wet of a receding wave. There at the ocean's hissing edge on a clear night you can throw a six-inch plug straight toward Portugal and if you're very careful you can see it land out there just before you flip the bail and bring it back, wiggling silent in the black water.

If the moon comes up, it's even prettier. Then you'll be tempted to put on a surface popper and you'll cast under the moon so you can drag the gurgler back, cutting a little vee-wake through the washed light.

It's lovely either way, and you might get a bit mesmerized by it, standing in that one place and casting repeatedly just to watch it happen. But you won't catch fish.

To catch fish you'll have to wait for another night, and you won't know for sure that the time is right until after dinner. It's a fine way to do it, actually. Inside the salt-greyed beach house the windows will be steamed from two hours of cooking and four hours of boasting; the sink will be crowded with clam and lobster shells, paper plates and beer cans; and fishermen of varying attitudes, physical and mental, will fill the room. Sometime after ten, Norb or Knowles or one of the other gung-ho types will step outside. When he comes back the wind will follow him in, cold and wet and moving paper napkins off the table.

"Perfect," he'll announce, wiping flecks of rain from his face. "Tide won't wait. Who's up?"

And about half the group will suit up—chest waders, wool sweaters, rain slickers—and organize themselves loosely into jeep-loads. It's six miles of macadam and seven of sand to the Point.

The Point. Here all the sandy edges of the island come together and fade into the sea like the trailing edge of a comma. When the tide slides up and out the west side, and the wind pushes in from the east side, you get what they call the "rip." If you were 18 inches tall, standing on the down-river end of a midstream sand bar on a windy night on the Porcupine River, you'd have the freshwater equivalent. Maybe.

Here in the ocean it must be dark, for it's then that the big gamefish, the striped bass and the bluefish, come over the sandbars. The water there is only a foot or two deep, roiled in a collision of wind and gravity, and the big fish come fast and hard from the depths on either side. There is no delicacy here—if your lure is there when the fish is there, the fish will eat it.

When the jeeps get to the Point, the group will fan out across and around the tip, feeling out the rip, blind casting into the gloom. You'll pick your own spot, standing as close to the water as you dare in the dark, and you'll cast, too.

You'll cast eagerly at first, tense on each retrieve, feeling for the fish, riding in spirit with the plug as it sails out over the wilding sea, retreating in spirit to let it swim alone in the black and lowering crosscurrents. After a while you'll settle down, allow the rhythm to set in. You know it may be hours until the schools come in to the beach, or it may be now, just now . . .

Bump.

Strike back. No. Nothing there.

The bumps are hard to read. *Doing anything?* someone will say. *Had a bump a while ago,* you'll answer. Who knows what it was? Maybe just the bottom, a quick drag through the sand, or maybe a slow-moving skate, nearly foul-hooked. Maybe a 25-pound bass.

But the fish are out there, somewhere out of casting range. Maybe just barely out of casting range. Maybe you should stand a little deeper into the breakers, go for it. You reach out with a tentative foot, feeling for the drop-off, for the soft, sliding sand that will collapse from under you on the first big wave. No fun to take a swim tonight. Firm sand, though, and a steady slope, so you take a few steps into the rip. Now the waves are breaking together just in front of you, slapping together and rolling up behind you to wash strong against your thighs on the outflow. Your face is wet now and when you lick your lips it's salt, not fresh, that's dripping off your nose. Plant your feet. Cast way out into it.

Now the tide is running harder, so that when your lure comes back to the beach it's ten yards to your right. The wind picks up, a pop-gust from the east, and you use it, leaning into a long, high cast out to the left of the rip. The wind will carry it for you, the tide will suck it back into the good water. You're sure of that. You can't see a thing.

You make a very slow retrieve, knowing that the rip will take care of the rest. You can feel the little tugs and runs as your plug is jostled into the confused water. More bumps, you smile to yourself. Must be getting shallow out there . . .

Bump.

Bump. *Pulllll!* Full bend. Line vanishing straight out into the rip. A big fish in very shallow water, panicked, running for the deep.

Afterward, later that night, and later in years when you have come to know it, you'll usually see it this way. West tide, east wind, very dark. At the tip end of Nantucket, where the sand curves into the sea. It's among the very best of memories: the kind where reminiscence is never very far from anticipation, in a place where even the land itself ends with the promise of a comma, and never the finality of a period.

May, 1981

This book was designed by
DeCourcy Taylor Jr.
The paper is Monadnock Text
Natural Laid
The type is Caslon 540 and was
set by DEKR Corporation,
Woburn, Massachusetts
The printing was by Daamen,
Inc., Center Rutland, Vermont
The binding was by New
Hampshire Bindery, Inc., Concord,
New Hampshire